Poetic Profiles of Faith

Poetic Profiles of Faith

by Tiffany L. Tolbert

Tiffany L. Tolbert Publishing
Atlanta, Georgia 30331
USA

Poetic Profiles of Faith
Copyright © 2007 by Tiffany L. Tolbert. All rights reserved.

All Scripture references cited in this text are taken from the King James Version (KJV) of the Holy Bible.

All material contained in this publication or any portion thereof may not be reproduced, stored in a retrieval system, transmitted or distributed in any form or by any means (electronic, recording, mechanical, photocopying, or otherwise) without prior written permission from the publisher of this book.

The scanning, uploading, and distribution of this book via the Internet or via any other means without the permission of the publisher is prohibited and punishable by law. Please purchase only authorized copies.

For more information, or to order copies, visit:
http://www.tiffanyltolbert.com

ISBN: 978-0-6151-4594-5

Cover & Interior Design by Tiffany L. Tolbert,
Copyright © 2007 Tiffany L. Tolbert

Author photograph © 2007 by Tiffany L. Tolbert

Printed in the United States of America.

To Julius.
The finest brother I could pray for,
God could make, and a mother and father could raise.

Contents

Acknowledgements	*ix*
Introduction	*xiii*

POETIC PROFILES

Reverend Dr. Martin Luther King, Jr.	1
Coretta Scott King	5
Mattie Stepanek	9
Mister Rogers	11
Oprah Winfrey	13
Tyler Perry	17
Jimmy Carter	21
Tavis Smiley	23
Bono	25
Rosa Parks	27
My Mother, My Father	29
S. Truett Cathy	33
Reverend Dr. James E. Hightower, Sr.	35
Dr. Benjamin S. Carson, Sr.	39
African-American Slaves	43

About the Author	47

Acknowledgements

*Mom, Dad, Sister and Brother:
There's an unnamed emotion, deeper than love, you give to me;
It helps me write. It helps me live.*

Matthew 17:20

*If ye have faith as a grain of mustard seed,
ye shall say unto this mountain,
Remove hence to yonder place; and it shall remove;
and nothing shall be impossible unto you.*

Introduction

The beginning of a successful life inaugurates at the very moment you align your thoughts and actions with those of God.

My big brother, an incredibly wise young man, stated to me again and again, *God gives every single person talents to use in life.* He'd explain, *Everyone's good at something; find what you enjoy doing and do it!* Talents are indeed allocated to everyone; they are spiritual gifts from God and act as a compass to His Will in our lives. They, combined with faith, induce the most supreme paths for us to trek; paths alluring order, paths alluring service and paths alluring completeness, freedom and joy.

The idea for this book came by surprise, as I sat idly. In a fated flash, everything clicked; everything my brother mentioned over and over finally made sense to me. Within seconds, I realized a talent I've been harboring for years was the inlet to my service; I realized my endowment from the Lord.

Poetic Profiles of Faith is a collection of poems depicting individuals, past and present, whose lives are pronounced testaments to the power of faith. These are persons who personify goodness, determination, persistence and courage; persons who had the option not to become who they are or do what they've done. Yet, they elected to utilize their endowments in positive ways, becoming successful; successful beyond measure, successful beyond wealth. With rhyming prose I honor their services, their forbearances, their triumphs, and their choice to illuminate: *All things are possible to him that believeth* (Mark 9:23).

Enjoy,
Tiffany L. Tolbert

Poetic Profiles of Faith

Reverend Dr. Martin Luther King, Jr.
Flagship Navigator
of the American Civil Rights Movement

The Constitution of the United States boasts the signatures of those deemed as the founding fathers of this great nation: George Washington, Benjamin Franklin, Thomas Jefferson and James Madison, Jr. among others. However, formed was a nation of inequality where all people were, in reality, not equal. Martin Luther King, Jr., in effect, was the founding father of the more perfect union, where the significance of skin color as a judgment of one's character was to be nonexistent.

• •

The embodiment of peace;
An example of ceaseless love,
It's impossible to look at Rev. King
and not know God's above.
Revealed through his words,
confirmed by his actions,
In opportunities to fight with fists and guns,
he fought with nonviolent reactions.

Blessed are the peacemakers:
They're children of the Lord (Matthew 5:9),
Such as King, who served tirelessly,
tirelessly for his Reward.
In the fearsome face of hatred,
and the irritation of deadly threats,

Dr. King kept going even when hard
got as hard as hard can get.
The epitome of utter faith
and the Lord's Will achieved,
King's vision was reachable for the reason:
He believed.

With much on his shoulders,
he walked upright, straight and steady,
Stared death in the pupil of its eyes;
He was armored, eager and ready.
He said a person with nothing to die for
is not fit to live,
Demonstrating love purges hate
was what he died to yield.

Using life for God's purpose,
he marched, he toiled, he strove;
Using talents from God for good,
a better future for the future he wove.

The most influential orator
in modern eras gone by,
His distinctive blend of bass and chime,
a remarkable battle cry.
When he talked masses listened;
In awe, they were mesmerized,
At such a man who'd insist on loving

even while being chastised.
He publicized to the nation,
and the globe, a harsh reality:
Ones bejeweled by darkened skin
were subjected to brutality.
King dared every one who observed,
not to rest while it went on,
He understood the fate of humankind,
all ethnicities it rests upon;
Peace in the north and west is tied
to peace in the south and east,
If hate is excused in one surrounding,
in others it will increase.

Dr. King highlighted the injuries
of equality's absence,
As midnight's sun;
A light made by God
aglowing verve and valiance.
A light made to drought injustice,
a light made to lead the world,
Dr. King was bravery, mental enormity,
and magnanimity furled.
He was a son, a brother, a husband,
a father, a chief, a friend,
Balancing family, movements,
and pastoring to earthly end.

The bullet that touched Martin Luther King, Jr., in essence, touched all countries, all over the world. His dream has helped to liberate more people in more places than any other vision ever articulated. Dr. King was an amazing servant of God for he never gave up:

He was arrested
b u t   k e p t   g o i n g …

He was criticized
b u t   k e p t   g o i n g …

He was stabbed
b u t   k e p t   g o i n g …

He was slandered
b u t   k e p t   g o i n g …

He was tired
b u t   k e p t   g o i n g …

He was murdered
a n d   y e t   h i s   l e g a c y   k e e p s   o n   g o i n g …

Through you and me.

Because of King and *Unsungs* before
we can let our freedom ring,
Because of their courage, pains and deaths
we're free to do our thing.

Coretta Scott King
Human Rights Activist & Leader

Wholeheartedly supporting racial, economic and gender justice, education, healthcare, and nonviolence, Mrs. Coretta Scott King was a highly regarded human rights activist and leader. Astute and artful, she also held interests and a Bachelor of Arts degree in Music and Education and studied concert singing at the New England Conservatory of Music in Boston, Massachusetts; there she earned an additional degree in Voice and Violin and first encountered her husband, Martin Luther King, Jr.

• •

It's inevitable man will die;
So that's not why,
if you see me cry, why I cry.
If I cry tears of sadness,
then I'll cry tears of joy,
Though she's departed, I'm eased,
she's in Heaven forevermore.

The land of all things pure,
that's where she now resides,
There with God Almighty
postured right beside her side.
Gazing the image of Him,
I know, she fell to her knees,

And reunited with her truelove-Martin,
dad-Obadiah, mom-Bernice.
In throngs shouting jubilantly,
draped in a white robe,
She's *singing* praises unto God,
and marching streets of gold.

So that's why,
if you see me cry, why I cry;
I know there's a better place for believers
upon the day they die.
And while earning my Heavenly rest
in the way the Lord will lead,
I'll muse upon her legacy,
her heap of selfless deeds.

For:
If poise had a proper name,
if heroism had a face,
If courage had a prototype
and love, a meeting place;
It was her.

Her strength provided hope,
possibilities and change,
Much in times when peace and unity
were blatantly estranged.
Her presence served as inspiration
and her life symbolizes,

That in walking with God,
over injustice, the just forever rises.
She's proof that beauty never fades,
integrity still remained,
And faith in God keeps one aligned
with steps He preordained.

If elegance was a being,
if intelligence had a heart,
If royalty and warmth
were wrapped together
to not ever come apart;
It was her.

Queen King.

Mattie Stepanek
"Poet, Peacemaker & Philosopher Who Played"

Although he succumbed to a rare form of muscular dystrophy at the age of thirteen, this self-described *poet, peacemaker and philosopher who played* lived a full, full life. Mattie Stepanek fulfilled all of his life wishes by becoming a published writer, meeting former President Jimmy Carter, and appearing on the *Oprah Winfrey Show*. As the best selling author of such books as *Reflections of a Peacemaker: A Portrait Through Heartsongs* and *Journey Through Heartsongs*, millions around the world have enjoyed reading and been inspired by his poetry. But what really made young Mattie's life so satiated was his faith in God; what mattered to him the most as a child, even more than fun and games, was praying prayers of peace, love and gratefulness.

• •

He was:
Bigger than his body
Deeper than his breathes
Stronger than his age
Rarer than his peace

Brighter than his outlook
Far-reaching than his smile
Wiser than his words
Sweeter than his *songs*

He is:

Lofty like his soul

Memorable as his faith

Mister Rogers

*Ordained Minister, Child Advocate, Writer, Producer,
Composer, Philanthropist &
TV Host of Mr. Rogers' Neighborhood*

Fred Rogers applied his passion for children and fervor for values toward the longest running Public Broadcasting Service programming in America, *Mister Rogers' Neighborhood*. Every airing began with him swapping a sweater and a pair of shoes, as he created an atmosphere on the small screen that would be beneficial in the development of young children's personalities. His collegiate studies in Music Composition and his natural proficiency as a puppeteer were valuable in composing the show's chorales and illustrative skits. *Neighborhood* currently runs in syndication conveying to a whole new generation that everyone is unique and special, and everyone can be just as good-hearted, regal and awe-inspiring as Mr. Rogers illustrated how to be.

• •

A lifetime of goodness
he sought to prepare,
For young children
who watched him on the air.

Television his tool, nurturing his goal,
In fostering imaginations
and cheering the soul.
Via kindness,

two sweaters and *two sets of shoes,*
Young lives were enriched
while being amused.
He taught viewers self worth,
educated their minds,
The gist of gentle, his actions defined.

In examining his faith—tenure and bare,
I look to Heaven incontestably aware.
His goal, accomplished; desire, fervent,
I can picture God saying,
Well done my servant (Matthew 25:23).

Oprah Winfrey
*Actress, Producer, Businesswomen, Humanitarian
& TV Host of the Oprah Winfrey Show*

Ms. Winfrey's life undoubtedly authenticates what she repeatedly declares: *God can dream a bigger dream for you than you can ever dream for yourself!* At the budding age of 19, she was making history as the youngest person and first Black American woman to anchor news at WTVF-TV in Nashville, Tennessee. Nowadays, she's following-up her historic introduction into television by flourishing as an entertainment pioneer in TV, movies, print and digital media, satellite radio and on Broadway. Long believing education is the passageway to furtherance, Oprah Winfrey, through charitable foundations like her own *Angel Network*, builds schools and youth centers, and subsidizes scholarships; overall, fostering environments across the world that are conducive to the actuation of dreams many have for themselves and those predestined in God's master plan.

••

In her mentions of faith,
Out rounds of her mirth,
In the depth of her doings,
I see what she is:
Complete. Contented. Compassionate.

She once said,
I'm easy to look at, but so hard to see...,

Well, judging from her aura,
I readily agree.
Just as it's easy to look at the sun's
radiance from a distance,
But so hard to see from gleaming rays,
is liken to her existence.

Perhaps luminosity comes
by all the joy she spreads,
Or by the bulk of her successes,
or the number of dreams she sets ahead.
Possibly sights can't view beyond
the love within her heart,
Or pass the progress she effectuates,
or the knowledge she imparts.
Maybe it's hard to see while counting
the obstacles she overcame,
Or while scanning the span of her intellect,
or the height of her inner aim.

Nevertheless; in truth, she is easy to see.

It's easy to see the enormous glee
her beloved image supplies,
And the sparkles of her magnetic presence,
daylight smile and warm eyes.
It's easy to see her innate exuberance,

and for others she truly cares,
It's easy to see
with all she has been blessed,
she willingly shares.
It's easy to see
wings on the *Angel Network*
and the halo of its head,
It's easy to see
how bettered mankind becomes
with her kindness being widespread.
It's easy to see every phase of her life
has been steps toward why she beams,
Evidence:
God's Will is bigger than any dream.

Inspiring.

Gifted.

Legendary.

Refined.

It's easy to see how she's a star,
For it's easy to see how bright she shines.

Tyler Perry
Playwright, Director, Screenwriter,
Composer, Producer, Actor, Author & Philanthropist

Inspired to alleviate woe through writing, Tyler Perry began inscribing expressions of his feelings and life experiences unto paper. These notes, ironically, served as a script for his first theatrical production, *I Know I've Been Changed*; a play referencing adult survivors of child abuse and the power of forgiveness. Though this stage play repetitively flopped over the next six years leaving him homeless at times, he clutched onto faith and did not give up. He kept working at his dreams, praying through stresses and difficulties for strength and navigation. At present, Mr. Perry has written more than 13 successful plays, movies and television shows, and still he is faithful. When major movie and television studios demanded his scripts abandon its religious connotations, he walked away; and in God's time, paraded into his own production studio complete with soundstages to film the many principled projects he continues to create.

• •

Congruent to *theatrical themes*,
His journey of realizing dreams.
From living rough to easy living,
From grasping grudges to full forgiving.

Directed by God through rendered *cues*
he trusted and followed through;

Through all the valleys and all the pain,
Through ups and downs
his faith remained.

Despite distress,
despite being afraid,
Despite repeated hardships,
on path he stayed.

Amid requests and orders
urging him to ponder quitting,
Perry decided to failure
he was not submitting.
His level of belief
exceeded that of doubt,
Optimism, drive—he dually held about.
Trusting in the Lord, he leaned to endure,
So the times he was fiscally broke,
he was never poor.

Protagonist—he's this story's hero,
He didn't allow setbacks to dictate
how far in life he'd go.
His survival *shows* what'll happen
if one can believe,
And *stages* anyone from anywhere
can carryout what they conceive.
His beginnings prepared him for now,
the next phases and the after,

As his artistic works reflect real life,
being filled with lessons and laughter.

Alike his works,
Mr. Perry heralds wisdom and motivation,
And alike his *plays*,
he's surely worthy of a *standing ovation*.

Jimmy Carter
Peacemaker, Humanitarian,
Author & Former President of the United States

Following his term as the 39th President of the United States of America, Jimmy Carter established *The Carter Center* to call attention to economic and social problems, to promote human rights and democracy, and to sponsor international conflict mediation; undertakings for which he was awarded the Nobel Peace Prize in 2002. His center also champions the extirpation of global diseases and discrimination against those with mental illnesses. This noted chef, amateur woodworker, Sunday School teacher, and painter has written nearly twenty two books and, together with his wife, Rosalynn, works with a number of charitable causes.

• •

Analogous to an autumn day;
Calm.   Cordial.   Colorful.
What's witnessed via scene and sound
is what's inside of him.

In him lies uniqueness
like the hues of fallen leaves,
A composure fused with fiber,
mixed with truth and peace.
His mediation and benevolence twinkle
through shade trees like the sun,
As a breeze refreshes air,

his works renew hope we'll all be one.
Faithful, altruistic, sedulous and inviting,
Are his motions, mood and languages—
in tongue and in writing.
The open skies are vast and clear
like that of his mentations,
Mentations channeling empathies
and harmonious aspirations.

Incited by a sermon preached
soon after his life began,
Angled: *If arrested, is there evidence
to indict you for being Christian?*
Conclusive clues have been harvested,
lots his life expose,
To charge him with being Jesus' own;
To declare his suit: Case Closed.

Tavis Smiley
Radio Host of The Tavis Smiley Show,
TV Host of Tavis Smiley, Author, Publisher & Philanthropist

In an effort to distance himself far from an abusive adolescent incident by the hands of his father, Tavis Smiley embarked on change. Foraging ahead, he graduated from Indiana University and established a career in radio and broadcasting, a career that lures many accolades recognizing his exceptional abilities to deliver news, talk and information. His leadership talents and philanthropy are also recognized, and applied to the *Tavis Smiley Foundation*, an organization that funds programs cultivating leadership in youth. Mr. Smiley is also a best-selling author with several books such as *Never Mind Success…Go for Greatness!* and his autobiography *What I Know for Sure: My Story of Growing Up in America*. From his profession he knows the importance of reporting fair and balanced news; from his life he knows that love always wins and faith is indispensable. He asserts the notion of belief into the psyche of viewers nightly on *Tavis Smiley*, signing off each broadcast with three immutable words: keep-the-faith.

• •

Abuse ignited his defeat of odds,
Proof all things work
for good in God (Romans 8:28).
Undeserved happenings,
he surpassed those does,
Arising unbeaten,

spiritually renewed;
What would have shattered
or crushed the halfhearted,
Prompted him to be stronger,
him to get started:
Opting for advancement,
abandoning what been,
Forgiving forebears,
proof *love wins*.

Never mind successful, he's labeled great,
As living proof of what comes
when folk *keep the faith*.

Bono
Musician & Humanitarian

Bono, one-fourth of the widely popular Irish rock band U2, has increasingly become involved in campaigning for third-world debt relief, and raising funds and awareness toward the obliteration of AIDS in Africa. He also travels globally crusading for cures of malaria and tuberculosis, and spearheads charitable operations that source foods, medicines and medical supplies to provinces where people cannot access what is needed to stay alive. These agilities are exactly why he was nominated for a 2003 Nobel Peace Prize; his faith is exactly why he's perseverant in caring for others in need.

••

His signature-styled sunglasses
can't shade the soul I see,
One connected with great concern,
goodwill and decency.
One comprised of first class love
for third world relief,
One championing a voice for *forgottens*:
The underprivileged and diseased.

As a man reared in faith
he gets everyone deserves the same,
Deliverance from scarcity,

sickness and solvable pain.
His committed labors improve,
planetary, the living of others,
Blessed is he that considereth the poor
(Psalm 41:1);
Beyond charity nothing's further
(1 Corinthians 13:13).

Through those lenses I see substance;
I respect what he pursues,
It's obvious that he loves the world;
Bono, the world loves *U 2*.

Rosa Parks
Mother of the Modern U.S. Civil Rights Movement

In 1955, Rosa Louise Parks began one of the most successful human demonstrations in United States history. By refusing to give up her seat to a white passenger on a Montgomery, Alabama, city bus as blacks were required to do, she refused any longer to be treated crudely because of her race. It wasn't she was more fatigued than usual after leaving her job as a seamstress and couldn't get up, it was that she'd grown extremely tired of suffering injustices. Conscious of the revengeful inflictions, confinements and threats that would come her way, she stood as she did anyhow, valiantly.

• •

By sitting Rosa stood
and keenly rearranged,
A society sickened, severely deranged.
Exhausted by prejudice: unjustifiable pain,
Mrs. Parks assembled rocks
into a boulder for change.

With rocks concealed in courage
and rocks congealed in faith,
The world availed
as racial barriers erased.
The claim for equal rights resumed
and revitalized,

As a result, disparities flattened,
new heights amplified;
Spiraling over torment
and ancestry segregations,
It s*eamed* a pattern for lasting,
unbiased transformations.

Exhausted by prejudice: unjustifiable pain,
Mrs. Parks assembled rocks
into a boulder for change.

My Mother, My Father
Happy 41st Wedding Anniversary

My parents, Robert & Louise Tolbert, have always furnished the lives of my siblings and me with priceless love and powerful sustenance. They are my greatest sources of inspiration, wisdom and support, and I, to the utmost degree, appreciate how they positively influence my ways of thought, manners, and speech. Through their lives and lifestyles I learned first handedly what faith is. I always knew God is real, God is good and God is able because I saw His spirit in their actions and His workings in their lives.

• •

The cornerstones of my heartbeat,
the air I breathe,
Nothing's worth more
in this world to me.
With a chance in choosing
my parents-to-be,
I would've chosen,
downrightly,
Robert and Louise.

The good in me extends
from the great they do,
And I pray as I grow older

their full worth I accrue.
They're archetypes
for how a man and a woman is,
In character, in faithfulness;
no shames, no fears.
They are solidly anchored,
singly and together:
Every daily encounter,
with the Lord God they endeavor.
They're a union made in loyalty,
compassion and in love;
One which marks me blessed,
one I'm so proud of.

In the very beginning they cared
as parents really should,
My sister, brother and I are grateful
they did all they could.
From helping with our homework
to the ills they helped to heal,
And fixing two green vegetables
with every nightly meal.
Interests in reading and learning,
they nourished and they fed,
They instilled into us morals
and by examples they both led.
When we were mistreated,
they rose to right the wrongs;

If we felt inferior,
they proclaimed we were just as strong.
Each Sunday, as a family,
they carried us to church,
So much tend was in our home,
in the world we did not search.
They wiped our tears, sourced hugs,
created curing smiles,
The stability and sense they added to life
presently compiles.

My parents,
the explanation of the balance in my life,
And the backing to look toward
when come bouts of strife.
They are cherished fortunes
God has given me,
Their leadership and devotion are
lasting guarantees.
They advise(d):
Never give up;
Obstacles can be a blessing,
Think positively,
in time you'll be progressing.
They repeatedly state,
Only believe, belief outcasts frustration,
Propelling fruition, voiding trepidation.
Not entirely perceiving their wisdom,

I chose to obey,
I'm glad,
I can't recall a time they led astray.

Each day I live, I'll tend to them,
repay I'll work to earn,
To show thanks for daily discipline,
sound judgment and concern.
Wherever they are,
no matter location, that will be my home,
There I'll find the love
that they have always shown.

Their unconditional parenting,
I with pleasure applaud,
I highly adore them both,
my greatest gifts from God.

S. Truett Cathy
*Founder & Chairman of Chick-fil-A, Inc.,
Author & Philanthropist*

S. Truett Cathy launched the first Chick-fil-A restaurant in 1946; thereafter, he and his brother created the boneless chicken sandwich, the eatery's signature menu item. And it's his devout belief in Christ that perforated Chick-fil-A's other signature feature: Closed Sundays. This course of action presents all employees the opportunity to attend church and spend quality time with their families. Mr. Cathy places his spirituality at the forefront of his personal and professional life; as a result, he's inwardly obliged to assist others in developing a better life. His corporation invests in scholarships, marriage seminars, character building programs and long term foster care for children. His faith is also vivid in Chick-fil-A's corporate purpose: *To glorify God by being a faithful steward of all that is entrusted to us and to have a positive influence on all who come in contact with Chick-fil-A.* Now that's good food for thought.

• •

As good as Chick-fil-A's foods taste,
And its fresh squeezed lemonade,
There's something better to rejoice,
Something not often portrayed,

S. Truett Cathy.

A businessman not for business,

Not obsessed with falling stocks,
A businessman that looks yonder funds,
One keen to Christian walk.

Committed to God through faith
and a steadfastness to serve,
Love is embedded deep in him
and visibly observed.
It's visible through his sincerities,
his habitual kindly acts,
All which makes a difference,
casting lasting impacts.
With a calling to strengthen families,
and a mission to care for youth,
He built a monopoly based on ethics,
on philanthropy and on Truth.

He's one of the most respectable,
world's richest men,
Accounted not by money
but his observance of the Word,
now and then.

Reverend Dr. James E. Hightower, Sr.
Pastor, Chaplain, College Dean
& Professor of Theology

To this day, James E. Hightower's face physically cringes at the eerie realization that he could have died unsaved while battling in World War II. Once returning home in 1946, he dedicated his life to God; presently, at the age of 83, he's been saved for over sixty years and is one of the oldest preachers actively pastoring. In addition to being a reverend, he has served for many years as a college professor, college dean, chaplain and president of Christian organizations. There are many exceptional qualities to Rev. Hightower, one being his appreciation for learning. After discharging from the US Army at age 23, he unashamedly enrolled as an eight grader to get an education; subsequently, he graduated from high school in the tenth grade and went on to garner a Ph.D., an academic degree of the highest level, in Divinity. A second and more noticeable trait is his unfaltering faith in God. At the age of 71, obeying the Lord, he resigned his position as pastor of a large and financially-stabled church to establish another. Many denounced this feat factoring his age and resources; yet Dr. Hightower demonstrated, as he has with sickness and other life obstacles, that with God all things are possible (Matthew 19:26) and God will never leave nor forsaken you (Hebrews 13:5). At the close of every Sunday service, he encourages the congregation of Greater Elizabeth Missionary Baptist Church, the church he established in his early seventies, to study their Bibles each day. Rev. Hightower knows with this practice comes secured knowledge of God's Word, along with an escalation in faith; an escalation to heights nearer the spiritual level he endorses and maintains.

• •

Every single Sunday,
from his heart,
the Word he preaches,
His life is a testimony;
He's proof of what he teaches.
His words and his actions,
his joy and judgment,
Are indicators of his love for God;
His worship is evident.

He's been walking with the Lord
for over 60 years,
And firmly declares,
with Him there are no fears.

He has had to stand alone;
He has had to give up gains,
But through and through he believed
and continued in Jesus name.
He has sacrificed and
he has weathered storms,
But he dares not worry,
knowing what God promised,

God performs.
He remains contented
regardless to circumstance,
Knowing from struggles and sufferings
God assures deliverance.
Proudly proclaiming,
God Is Love and God Loves Us,
He speaks on the danger of unbelief
and stress in the Saviour trust.
He says, *Jesus responds to me*
according to my faith in Him,
And *the Lord is with us, for us*
whether times are great or grim.
He enunciates confidently
with class and clarity:
Seeking first the Kingdom of Heaven
is the real meaning of prosperity.

Absorbing his loyal allegiance each week
inspires a better being,
In witnessing he's fully guided by faith,
not by man, not by seeing.
He genuinely loves the Lord
and with Him are abound,
He's clearly Holy Spirit led,
Christ-centered and Heaven bound.

Dr. Benjamin S. Carson, Sr.
Neurosurgeon, Professor, Philanthropist & Author

By requiring her child to read daily, Sonya Carson augmented the outcome of her son Benjamin's life: he went from performing poorly in the fifth grade to reaping in the twelfth grade a scholarship to Yale University, and has since become one of the leading pediatric neurosurgeons in the world. It was through the routine of reading that Dr. Carson comprehended learning's relevance on success. Hence, he's made a personal commitment to forwarding the worth of education onto others, especially young persons. He shares his knowledge through the books he's written: *Gifted Hands*, *Think Big*, and *The Big Picture*; motivational speaking; and the *Carson Scholars Fund*, in which Dr. & Mrs. Carson encourages students to acquire high levels of academics by rewarding their yearn for excellence with grants to four year colleges and universities.

• •

A gifted man with *gifted hands*,
A gifted smile,
A gifted heart;
A gifted man with gifted eyes,
A gifted sane,
A gifted smart.

A gifted man with gifted aims,
A gifted stance,

A gifted vow;
A gifted man with gifted words,
A gifted past,
A gifted now.

A man who urges everyone's gifted,
blessed by the Lord,
With talents that should not be disowned,
pushed aside or ignored.
A man blessed with hands to mend,
a smile to comfort, a heart to care,
And gifted eyes that visualize
the revelations of unawares.
A man who thinks brilliantly,
with a sound wit and leveled head,
A mastermind who's well-balanced,
well-educated and well-read.

A man who *thinks big*,
brainstorming the inconceivable,
Then pursues and triumphs,
affirming aims are achievable.
A man who believes in God,
who believes in doing best,
A man who trusts when you do your best,
God will do the rest.
A man who prays at the start of day
for strength and for direction,

A man who's meek and honest;
A man of prized perception.
A man of hope and joy,
a man of morals and of peace,
A man whose faith doesn't waver
…rupture … or cease.
A man who honors youth
by extending them a chance,
To apply their skills and talents;
an opportunity he grants.
A man who expresses love
for his wife, his sons and patients,
A man who praises his mother
for her rules and regulations.
A man who explains the value
of employing one's potential,
In verbalizing *the big picture*:
Gifts and goodness are life's essentials.

A man from a boy in poverty,
poor grades and attitude,
Who grew to conquer crests
and carve new altitudes.
A man who exalts integrity
and zeal to beat the odds,
And testifies all that's needed
is belief in self and in God.

African-American Slaves
Slavery in North America

The enslavement of African-American people lapsed 240 years; the Thirteenth Amendment to the US Constitution officially abolished slavery in 1865. These slaves were the descendants of millions of Africans that were forcibly dragged from their homes, chained and crammed aboard ships traveling to North America. The vast majority of them were made to work on plantation fields harvesting crops as cotton, sugar, tobacco and rice while others worked inside the slave-owner's home cooking, cleaning and caring for the owner's family. Through it all, African-American slaves depended on the indiscriminate Grace of God. Although their faith rested in the same Being their owners believed in, they were restricted from openly worshipping the Lord; hence, they conceived Negro spirituals, hymns that conveyed their prayers and praises in a manner that only they knew what was expressed. Furthermore, the version of Christianity they embraced encompassed God's love for all mankind and His biblical deliverances of people out of tyrannical conditions; conditions in which they lived.

• •

Out of pain,
The nastiest pain,
pain of the cruelest kind,
Arose faith;
Faith at its finest,

Faith at its reason.

Out the midst of torments and sorrows
escalated rich, expressive hopes,
And the appetite to survive
in view of chains and lynching ropes.
Out the midst of chronic woes
escalated joy and tastes of free,
Through prayers and songs
intolerable plunged,
morphing to jubilee.
Forbidden to read or write,
they hummed, they sung, they prayed,
Vocally versing hymns of faith,
giving to God the praise.
Jesus died for everyone;
they knew this meant them too,
They knew that Jesus cared,
thus would bring them through.

In the midst of physical sufferings,
in weather so hot, so cold to stand,
Slaves were forced to work past worn,
past blood streaming down cuts in hands.
Past opened, bleeding flesh wounds
ripped by leather whips,
Past tortures, imprisonment
and freedoms stripped:

They hummed. They sung. They prayed.

In the midst of wrists tied tight
to trees stretched up high,
To be beaten unendingly,
and harmed by dogs until they died;

In the midst of being starved to death,
or worshipping God in code;
In the midst of being treated like things:
Inspected, traded and sold;
In the midst of being separately sold
from family to see no more,
In the midst of enduring sans the love
never done without before;

In the midst of limbs chopped off
with a mucky, metal axe;
In the midst of feeling remorse
from orders to thrash their friends' backs;
In the midst of being burnt alive,
raped, belittled and killed;
In the midst of fields containing crops
they planted, plucked and tilled;
In the midst of being shackled,
hated and buried alive;
In the midst of being overworked,
overwhelmed and tyrannized:

They hummed. They sung. They prayed.

Though born into slavery,
they departed into freedom,
To subsist with Mighty God,
eternally in the Kingdom;
They fiercely held to faith,
so they, out of bondage,
Were emancipated by the One,
unto the One they paid homage.
In Heaven there exist no hatred,
there lies no pain,
Love, peace and equality
everlastingly remain.

Out of pain,
The nastiest pain,
pain of the cruelest kind,
Arose tomorrow;
The tomorrows of mankind.
Out the midst of torments and sorrows
escalated models of Godly pride,
Models of hope and wisdom,
and overcoming uneasy stride.
Slaves braved inconceivable grief
while sturdily paving the way,
Their afflictions placed this world closer
to where it is today.

About the Author

Tiffany L. Tolbert has been creating poetry for more than sixteen years. Her first poems focused on social issues affecting adolescents.

She has worked with world renowned television news networks, acting troupes, and several local news publications; all which have contributed to her ability to nurture creative projects. In addition to writing poetry, she also enjoys penning songs, short narratives and speeches, and designing specialty programs, fliers and greeting cards.

A graduate of Georgia State University with a Bachelor of Science degree in Biology, Tiffany was born, raised and currently resides in Atlanta, Georgia.

www.tiffanyltolbert.com

www.ingramcontent.com/pod-product-compliance
Lightning Source LLC
LaVergne TN
LVHW011413080426
835511LV00005B/519